THE
OBOE SOLOIST

To access audio visit:
www.halleonard.com/mylibrary

Enter Code
5124-1943-1978-9025

ISBN 978-1-59615-351-6

Music Minus One

EXCLUSIVELY DISTRIBUTED BY

HAL•LEONARD®
7777 W. BLUEMOUND RD. P.O. BOX 13819 MILWAUKEE, WI 53213

Visit Hal Leonard Online at
www.halleonard.com

CONTENTS

Aria
St. Matthew Passion

JOHANN SEBASTIAN BACH
(1685-1750)

5 taps plus 1 silent
precede music.

Sonata in A Minor

4 taps (1 measure)
precede music.

I

GEORG PHILLIPP TELEMANN
(1681-1767)

II

6

4 taps (2 measures)
precede music.

IV

Vivace

Piano enters on upbeat of 2nd beat
in 2nd measure after letter D.

Largo

8 taps (1 measure) precede music

JOHANN FRIEDRICH FASCH
(1688-1758)

Concerto No. 8 in Bb

I

GEORGE FRIDERIC HANDEL
(1685–1759)

Adagio ♪ = 80

II

Allegro

III

Siciliana

IV

6 taps (2 measures) precede music.

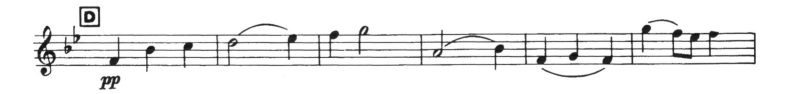

Andante and Allegro

from: Sonata No. 15

3 taps (1 measure) precede music.

JEAN-BAPTISTE LOEILLET
(1680-1730)

Andante

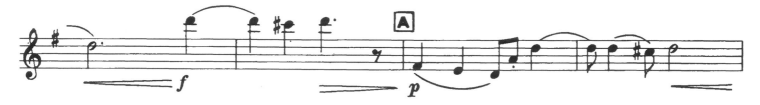

Romance No. 1

from: Three Romances

3 taps (1 measure) precede piano entrance.

ROBERT SCHUMANN, Op. 94
(1810-1856)

Moderato ♩ = 100

Dreams
(Träume)

RICHARD WAGNER
(1813-1883)

Two Songs

I
It must be wonderful, withal

FRANZ LISZT
(1811–1886)

II
Joyful and Woeful

Theme
Symphony in C, 2nd Movement

GEORGES BIZET
(1838–1875)

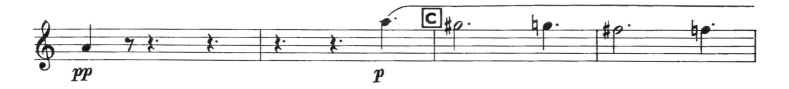

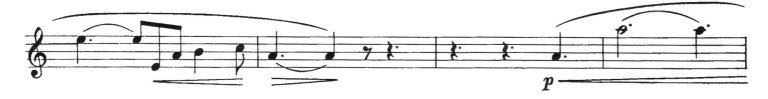

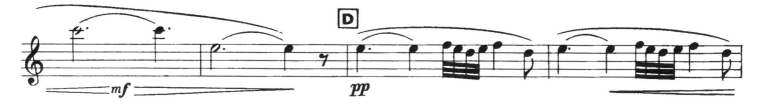

Two Arabian Dances

I

Andante con moto quasi allegretto ♪ = 144

MAX LAURISCHKUS, Op. 3
(1876–1929)

18

II

Mazurka

CLAUDE DEBUSSY
(1862-1918)

Vocalise

SERGEI RACHMANINOFF, Op. 34, No. 14
(1873–1943)

4 taps (1 measure) precede music.

Lentamente e molto cantabile

Song

REINHOLD GLIÈRE, Op. 35, No. 3
(1875-1956)

Kuruka-Kuruka

KÕSÇAK YAMADA (1886-   )
Arranged by W.T.

p con morbidezza

mp

p con morbidezza

mf

mp

p

pp

Toadinha
(A Little Song)

JEAN BERGER (1901-   )
Arranged by W.T.